BIBLE BULLETIN
FOR HOLI

by
Dee Leone

illustrated by
Janet Armbrust

Cover by Teresa Mathis

Copyright © 1994

Shining Star Publications

ISBN No. 0-86653-777-5

Standardized Subject Code TA ac

Printing No. 9876

Shining Star
A Division of Frank Schaffer Publications, Inc.
23740 Hawthorne Boulevard
Torrance, CA 90505-5927

Unless otherwise indicated, the New International Version of the Bible was used in preparing the activities in this book.

TO THE TEACHER

Bible Bulletin Boards for Holidays will make decorating your boards for the holidays happy and hassle-free. Forty-six pages of holiday patterns and an equal number of bulletin board ideas make this a book you'll use all through the year. You'll find ideas for New Year's, Valentine's Day, Easter, Thanksgiving, Christmas, and many other holidays. There are valuable suggestions for extending the bulletin board themes with books, crafts, songs, prayers, and readings. And the best thing of all is that children take an active part in the creation of each and every bulletin board!

Patterns are provided to help you and your children create the most important part of each display. These patterns may also be used for art projects, work sheets, greeting cards, awards, invitations, notices, and posters. The Bible verse given below each bulletin board picture may be written on one of the patterns or incorporated elsewhere in the display.

The backgrounds, borders, and letters for the bulletin board captions may be as simple or as elaborate as desired. You may want to display the patterns on a traditional paper background, or experiment with the background of foil, wrapping paper, fabric, newspaper, shelf liner, or colored adhesive plastic. Letters may also be cut from any of these materials. In additon, you may want to try decorating letters with dots, stripes, designs (outline with black marker), or holiday stickers. Another option is to make some of the letters into a design that fits the bulletin board theme. An "O" for example, could become a balloon, wreath, face, coin, or piece of candy. Let your imagination soar!

So, use the ideas in this book, combined with the children's creations and your imagination, and the end result will be a year's worth of holiday bulletin boards that are beautiful and truly unique!

My friends through the holidays and through the years.

TABLE OF CONTENTS

Shining Star Publications, Copyright © 1994
SS3810

HAPPY NEW YEAR!

MAKE A JOYFUL NOISE
TO THE LORD

Verse: "This is the day the Lord has made; let us rejoice and be glad in it."

Psalm 118:24

Patterns: Make several copies of the favors on page 6. Have the children write verses about rejoicing and praising God on them. Possible verses include Psalms 81:2; 81:3; 100:1; 108:1; 118:24; Proverbs 15:15; and Philippians 4:4. When children have memorized the verse written on a favor, they may color and cut out the party favor to add to the board.

Board: Display the party favors against a background of brightly colored, curled ribbon and confetti. Real party favors may be used to decorate the board and border. Children may remove them as rewards for memorizing verses, replacing them with ones they've made.

Activity: Have the children cover a short cardboard tube with colorful wrapping paper or adhesive plastic. A few pennies, buttons, paper clips, bells, or other noisemakers may be inserted before a cardboard circle is taped over each end. Streamers may be added to both ends, and the completed rhythm instruments can be used when singing joyfully to the Lord.

Songs: "Sing a New Song"
"This Is the Day"

PARTY FAVORS

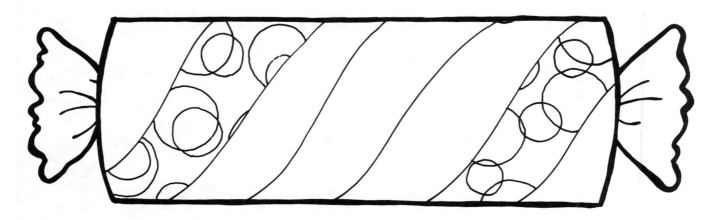

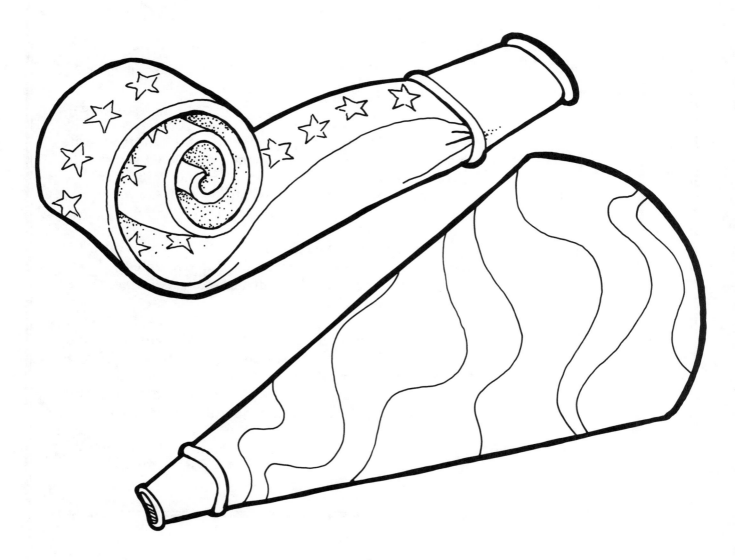

SS3810

RESOLVE TO MAKE THIS A BANNER YEAR

Verse: "God is with you in everything you do."   Genesis 21:22b

Patterns: Have children color and cut out the patterns on page 8. On their balloons, children may write their resolutions. On the hats, children may write Bible verses that remind them to stick to their resolutions. Possibilities include Matthew 19:26; Psalm 116:14; Psalm 119:59; Ephesians 4:24; and Philippians 3:14.

Board:  Write the caption on a colorful paper banner. Arrange the balloons and hats below it. Place some tape and an envelope full of 1" squares of tissue paper near the board. Let each child add a tissue paper square to the board each day his resolution has been kept. When the envelope is empty, celebrate by having a late New Year's party. (An option is to write classroom goals, such as remembering homework and being silent in the library, on the balloons. Each child meeting a goal may add a piece of confetti to the board.)

Activity: Children may write their resolutions on thin strips of paper and insert them in real balloons. These may be blown up and taken home to remind the children not to "break" their balloon resolutions.

Prayer: Dear God, help me to stick to my resolutions, and if I get off track, give me the strength to try again.

8

SS3810

NEW YEAR'S DAY

IT'S TIME TO

"At midnight I rise to give you thanks."
Psalm 119:62a

RING IN THE NEW YEAR

Verse: "There is a time for everything, and a season for every activity under heaven."
Ecclesiastes 3:1

Pattern: Copy the clock on page 10 for each child. On the clock base, each child should write something she feels it is time to do, such as read the Bible every day, count her blessings, or start eating right. The clocks may then be colored, cut out, and added to the board.

Board: Use an overhead projector to enlarge the clock for the center of the board. Write the words of Psalm 119:62a on the clock base. Mount the children's clocks around the large one. Add bells or party favors for the border.

Activity: Set an alarm clock to go off at various times during the day. At those times, select some students to rise and give thanks to God for things that happened during the past year.

Reading: Ecclesiastes 3:1-8

Shining Star Publications, Copyright © 1994

SS3810

IT'S TIME TO:

NEW YEAR'S DAY

A NEW YEAR— A NEW GIFT FROM GOD

God has given me a new year to use as I will.
I can use it to grow and to find needs to fill,
Or instead, I can idly waste it away
Doing nothing important with each passing day.
When this year is gone I hope I can say
That the life I exchanged for it was a good price to pay.

Verse: "The gift of God is eternal life in Christ Jesus our Lord." Romans 6:23b

Patterns: Copy the calendar and bow on page 12 for each child. Each child may cut out the calendar and decorate it with the bow to look like a gift. A snowflake, mitten, or other winter sticker or drawing may be added to the calendar each day the child performs a special service, such as reading to a younger child or visiting someone who is lonely.

Board: Cut the letters for the caption from wrapping paper. Place a wrapped box or a picture of a large gift in the center of the board. Decorate it with a bow and a tag that says "To: Me, From: God." Enlarge the poem and place it on the package. Add the children's calendars to the board and decorate the border with bows and the year.

Activity: A whole year's worth of calendar sheets may be stapled together for each child. Stickers or drawings symbolic of the month may be used each day the child performs a good deed.

Prayer: Help me to remember that each day is a gift from You, God, and help me to live each day accordingly.

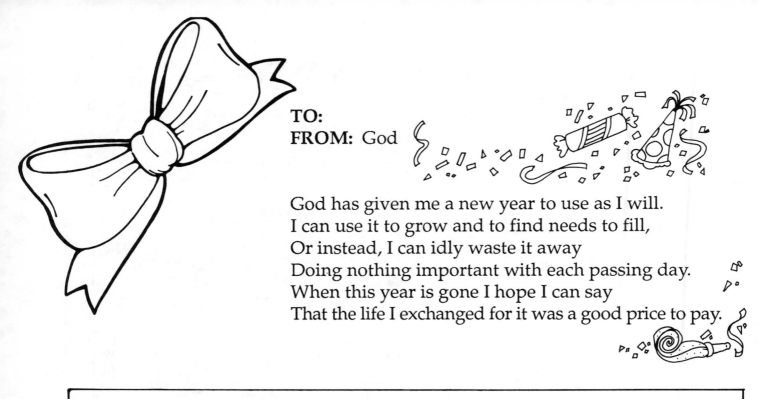

TO:

FROM: God

God has given me a new year to use as I will.
I can use it to grow and to find needs to fill,
Or instead, I can idly waste it away
Doing nothing important with each passing day.
When this year is gone I hope I can say
That the life I exchanged for it was a good price to pay.

S	M	T	W	T	F	S

SS3810

MARTIN LUTHER KING, JR. DAY

I, TOO, HAVE A DREAM

Verse: "He had a dream in which he saw a stairway resting on the earth, with its top reaching to heaven, and the angels of God were ascending and descending on it." Genesis 28:12

Pattern: Copy the pattern on page 14 for each child. The child may color and cut out the ladder and decorate it with silver glitter. On the cloud, he may write a dream for his future or the future of the world. Discuss how children can help the dreams come true.

Board: Cut the letters for the caption from aluminum foil. Arrange the ladders among silver stars and cotton balls stretched out to resemble clouds.

Activity: Talk about Martin Luther King, Jr. and his "dream." Read and discuss some dreams the Bible mentions, such as Jacob's dream in Genesis 28, Joseph's dreams in Genesis 37, the dreams of the cupbearer and baker in Genesis 40, and the Pharaoh's dreams in Genesis 41.

Book: *Martin Luther King, Jr.: The Story of a Dream* by June Behrens, 1979, Children's Press.

SS3810

I HAVE A DREAM

14

REACH OUT AND TOUCH SOMEBODY'S HAND

Verse: "If we love one another, God lives in us and his love is made complete in us." 1 John 4:12b

Pattern: Make several copies of the heart pattern on page 16, color them, and write a different verse about love or brotherhood on each one: John 13:34; 1 John 4:19; 1 John 4:20; Luke 10:27; and 1 Corinthians 13:13. Cut each heart into puzzle pieces, and place the pieces in an envelope.

Board: Use an overhead projector to enlarge the heart. Color it red and white and cut it out. Let children trace their hands on paper of many colors to create the rainbow effect of a brotherhood of different peoples. Have the children cut out the hands and mount them around the heart so that they are touching. Tack the puzzle envelopes to the board. Add paper dolls made from the patterns on page 68.

Activity: Let children put the heart puzzles together. In addition, envelopes and pen pal address cards may be put near the board to encourage children to "reach out and touch someone" in another land. This board may also be used for United Nations Day on October 24.

Songs: "Reach Out and Touch Somebody's Hand"
"Up, Up with People"
"What the World Needs Now Is Love, Sweet Love"

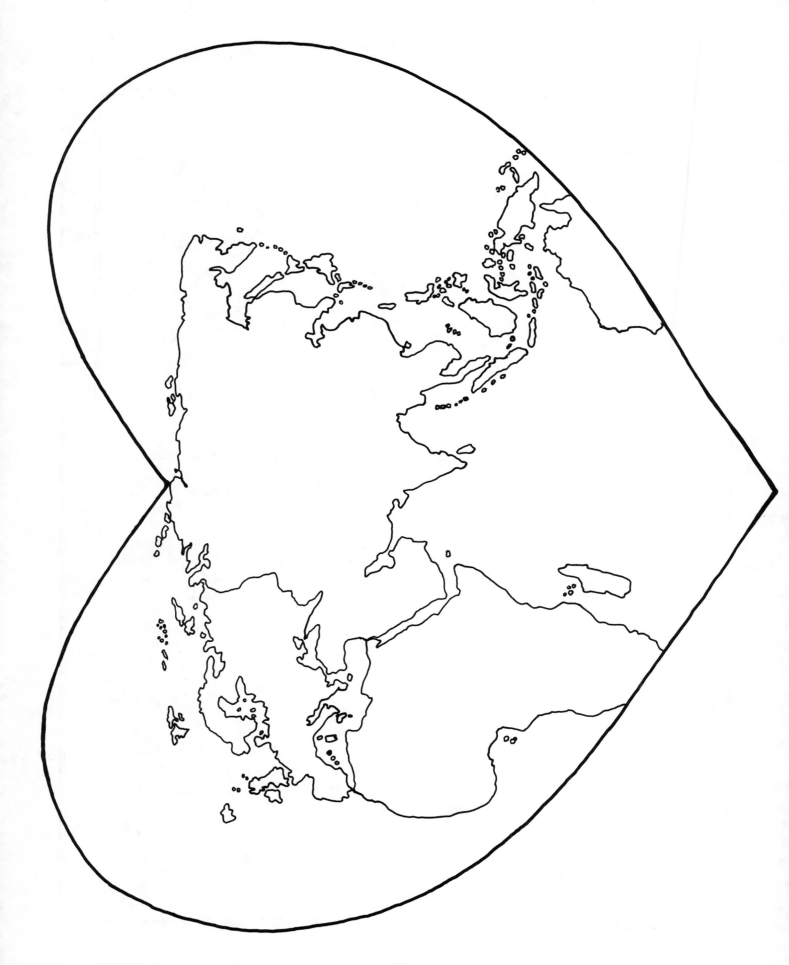

16

BIBLICAL VALENTINES

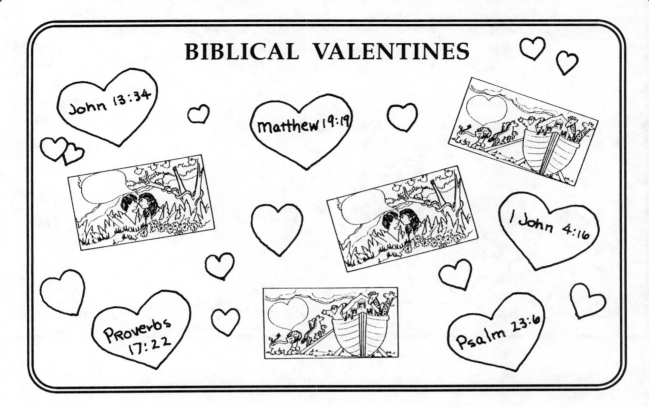

Verse: "A cheerful heart is good medicine."   Proverbs 17:22a

Patterns: Make copies of the valentines on page 18 for children to color and cut out, adding greetings to match the scenes pictured. (Examples: Adam and Eve–You're the only one for me./I'll be in paradise if you'll be my valentine. Ark Animals–There'll be brighter days ahead if you'll be my valentine.)

Board: Mount the biblical valentines on the board with paper hearts that have love verses written on them. Add valentine stickers to the border.

Activity: Encourage children to create their own biblical valentines to add to the board. They may wish to use scenes showing Jesus and the children, a lion and a lamb, etc. In addition, have children hunt through the Bible for verses containing the word "love." Award valentine stickers to the ones who find the most in ten minutes. Then encourage them to write some of the verses on paper hearts to be displayed on the board.

Reading: 1 Corinthians 13:1-13

NOAH'S ARK VALENTINE

ADAM AND EVE VALENTINE

JESUS LOVES ME

Verse: "Let the little children come to me . . . ."   Mark 10:14b

Pattern: Give each child a copy of the heart on page 20 to color and cut out. Put a photo of the child on the heart. An option is to cut out magazine pictures of children of various races to put on the hearts. The caption should then read "JESUS LOVES THE LITTLE CHILDREN."

Board: Use an overhead projector to enlarge the picture of Jesus and the children for the center of the board. Color it, mount it on the board, and then arrange the children's photo hearts around it.

Activity: Children may use the hearts to make Valentine's Day cards. Make copies of the picture of Jesus to be glued to the outside of construction paper cards. The heart can be glued to the inside. The word YOU may be added to the hearts under the words JESUS LOVES. The valentines should be given to special friends.

Songs: "Jesus Loves Me"
"Everything Is Beautiful"

JESUS LOVES...

20

VALENTINE'S DAY

"A HAPPY HEART MAKES THE FACE CHEERFUL." Proverbs 15:13a

Verse: "A happy heart makes the face cheerful."   Proverbs 15:13a

Pattern: Make a copy of the clown on page 22 for each child to color, cut out, and decorate with yarn, stickers, sequins, etc. The clowns may be mounted on paper hearts with the words "I'M NOT JUST CLOWNING AROUND . . . I WANT YOU FOR MY VALENTINE."

Board: Use clown or balloon wrapping paper as the background on which to arrange the clowns. Small paper balloons, clown hats, or bow ties may be used as a border.

Activity: Parent volunteers or older children may help each child to literally put on a happy face with the use of face-painting materials. Let the child choose to have valentine symbols or a clown face painted on. Children may sing "If You're Happy and You Know It" or "Put on a Happy Face."

Book: *The Clown of God* by Tomie de Paola

SS3810

22

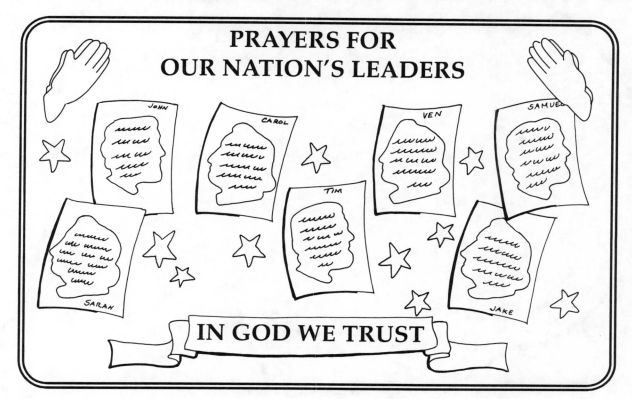

PRAYERS FOR OUR NATION'S LEADERS

IN GOD WE TRUST

Verse: "God reigns over the nations."   Psalm 47:8a

Patterns: Each child may write a prayer for our nation's leaders on one of the patterns which you have copied from page 24. The patterns may be cut out and mounted on half sheets of red or blue construction paper.

Board: Red and white striped letters may be used for the caption. Mount part of the words on a blue paper banner. Display the children's prayers with symbols pertaining to the holiday. Bible verses related to leadership may be written on scrolls and added to the display. Appropriate verses include Psalm 47:8; Psalm 118:7; Psalm 119:106; 2 Chronicles 13:12; and 2 Chronicles 19:9.

Activity: Encourage children to examine coins and currencies for the words "In God We Trust." In addition, help them learn the identity of the President on each coin or bill.

Reading: Matthew 22:15-22

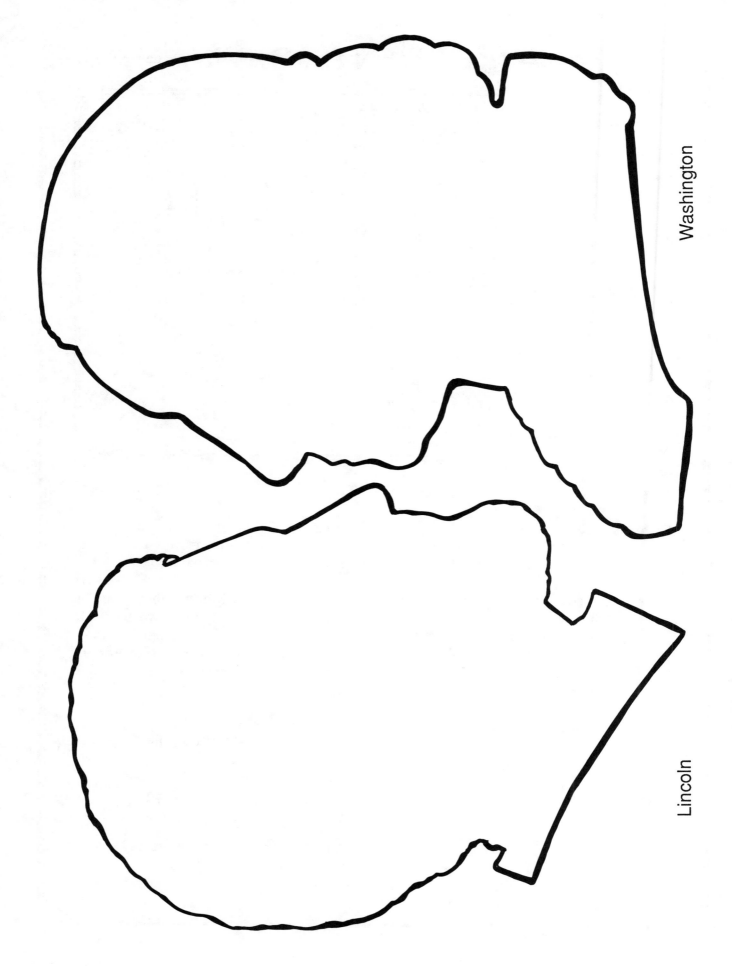

Washington

Lincoln

24

MAY THE LORD BLESS YOU AND KEEP YOU

An Irish Blessing

*May the road
rise up to meet you.
May the wind be
always at your back.
May the sun shine
warm upon your face,
The rains fall soft
upon your fields,
And until we meet again,
May God hold you
in the hollow of His hand.*

Verse: "May God be gracious to us and bless us and make his face shine upon us."
Psalm 67:1

Patterns: Copy the patterns on page 26 for each child. After reading "An Irish Blessing," children may color it and cut it out. Then have them write their own blessings on shamrocks cut from green paper.

Board: Use an overhead projector to enlarge "An Irish Blessing" for the board. Display the children's shamrocks around the blessing.

Activity: Make extra copies of the patterns. On both sides of the shamrock have each child list green blessings from God, such as grass, trees, or frogs. Challenge them to think of one for each letter of the alphabet. Encourage the children to use the blessing as part of a greeting card.

Songs: "A Song of Blessing"
"The Peace of the Lord"

SS3810

An Irish Blessing

May the road
rise up to meet you.
May the wind be
always at your back.
May the sun shine
warm upon your face,
The rains fall soft
upon your fields,
And until we meet again,
May God hold you
in the hollow of His hand.

SS3810

Verse: "Do not store up for yourselves treasures on earth . . . But store up for yourselves treasures in heaven." Matthew 6:19-20a

Patterns: Copy the pot on page 28 for each child to trace on black paper, cut out, and write her name on. Copy the coins on page 30, and write a Bible verse you would like the children to memorize on each. Appropriate verses include Matthew 13:44; Genesis 9:13; and Matthew 6:19-20. Make copies of the coins on yellow paper for children to take home. Each time a child memorizes a verse on one of the coins, she may cut out the coin and bring it back to pin or tape to her bulletin board pot.

Board: Make the word RAINBOW from several different colors and the other words from green or gold. Use an overhead projector to enlarge the pot for the board. Enlarge the coins on page 30, write Bible verses on them, and place them in the pot. Paint a rainbow coming out of the pot. Across the bottom of the board, add shamrocks made from the pattern on page 26. Display the children's pots to the side.

Activity: Hide some paper coins with verses on them for a treasure hunt. Then have the children seek God's Word.

Readings: Matthew 6:19-24 and parables of the kingdom in Matthew 13.

 SS3810

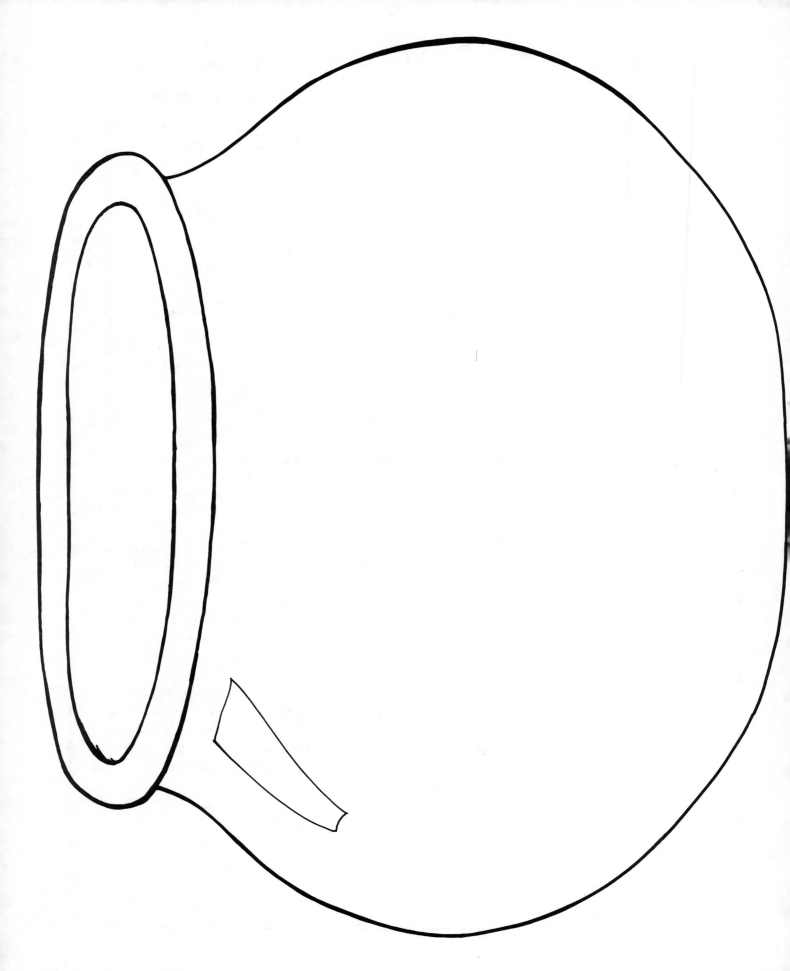

28

COUNT YOUR BLESSINGS

Verse: "May your blessings be on your people."   Psalm 3:8b

Patterns: Reproduce the coins on page 30 on yellow paper, or have the children color them before cutting them out. Have each child write a blessing received on a coin. Children may place their coins in individual pots made from the pattern on page 28 or in one large pot on the board.

Board: Use an overhead projector to enlarge the rainbow on page 42. Beneath it, display each child's small pot of gold or one large pot made from the pattern on page 28. Add a row of shamrocks made from the pattern on page 26.

Activity: Read and discuss the following Bible passages that contain special blessings: the blessing of Abraham in Genesis 12, Isaac's blessing in Genesis 27, and Jacob's blessing in Genesis 48-49. Divide the children into groups to act out some of the passages as skits.

Songs: "A Song of Blessing"
               "Glory and Praise to Our God"

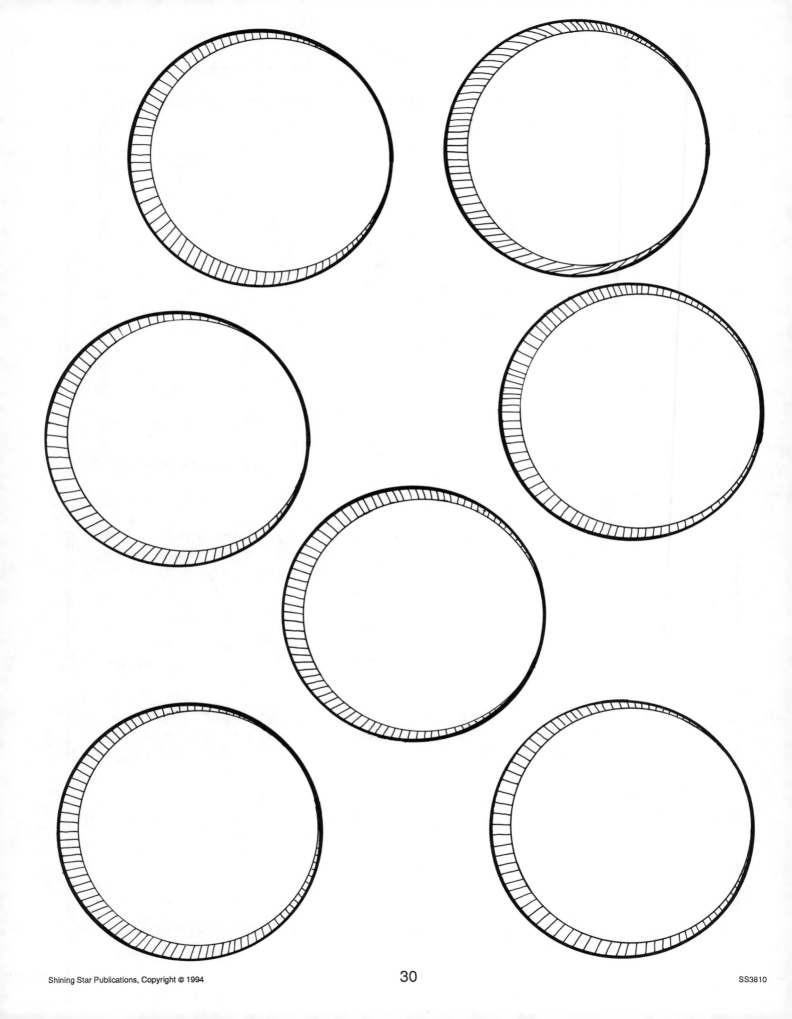

30

SS3810

LORD, HELP ME TO CHANGE AND GROW

Verse: "Therefore, if anyone is in Christ, he is a new creation; the old has gone, the new has come!" 2 Corinthians 5:17

Patterns: Copy the patterns on page 32 for children to color, cut out, and write their names on. On the back of the wings, each child should write a sacrifice or change he will make during the weeks before Easter. (Examples: I will give my allowance and snack money to missions. I will pray for a different person in my class each day. I will try to control my temper.)

Board: Mount the caterpillars on the board. On Easter, after children have fulfilled their promises, they may add wings to the caterpillars to transform them into beautiful butterflies.

Activity: Encourage children to use the weeks before Easter as a time to think about the sacrifice Jesus made for us and to focus on ways to change and grow closer to God. In addition, help them become more aware of the changes in nature going on around them. If possible, arrange for the children to observe the stages in the life cycle of a butterfly.

Prayer: God grant me the serenity to accept the things I cannot change, the courage to change the things I can, and the wisdom to know the difference. (Author unknown)

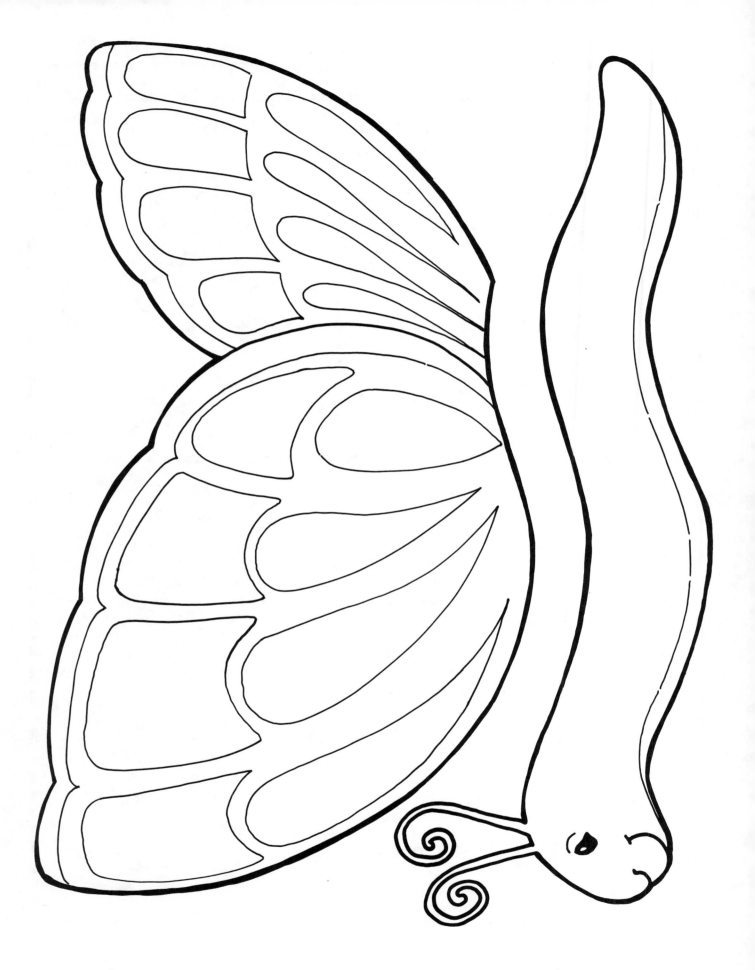

SS3810

SING HOSANNA!

SHOUT FOR JOY; YOUR KING IS COMING!

Verse: " . . . Hosanna to the Son of David! Blessed is he who comes in the name of the Lord. Hosanna in the highest! "   Matthew 21:9

Patterns: Make green copies of the palm branch on page 34, or give each child a palm branch to color green before writing his name on it. Reproduce the musical notes on page 34 using a variety of colors.

Board: Use an overhead projector to enlarge the picture of Jesus shown above. Mount it at the center of the board. Add the caption, the children's palm branches, and the musical notes.

Activity: Have children sing songs of praise while waving their palm branches in joyful anticipation of the coming of Jesus. Then read of His triumphal entry in Luke 19:28-44. Discuss the words of Jesus to the Pharisees who asked Him to quiet the disciples. "I tell you," He said, "if they keep quiet, the stones will cry out." Then have each child paint a smooth stone with the word HOSANNA and palm branches or other Easter symbols.

Song: "Sing Hosanna"

34

SS3810

A GARDEN OF PRAYERS

Verse: " . . . May your will be done." Matthew 26:42

Patterns: Copy the flowers on page 36. Have children write brief prayers on them, asking God to help them fulfill Easter promises. (Examples: Dear God, help me to say only nice things about others. O Lord, help me to be willing to set aside more time for Bible study.) Let children color the flowers and cut them out.

Board: Use an overhead projector to enlarge the picture of Jesus shown above. Letters for the caption may be cut from floral wallpaper or shelf liner. Choose at least one flower from each child to add to the display.

Activity: Have each child illustrate a scene from Jesus' last days, such as Jesus before Pilate, washing the disciples' feet, praying in the garden, or carrying the cross.

Prayer: Say the "Lord's Prayer" together in a garden setting.

Verse: "Jesus said, 'Father, forgive them, for they do not know what they are doing.' "   Luke 23:34a

Pattern: Copy the pattern on page 38 for each child. Have the child place it on a paper towel and use a cotton ball to coat it with mineral or cooking oil to make the paper more translucent. After each Bible verse the child memorizes, he may use a crayon to color all the corresponding coded parts. When all parts have been colored, a black crayon or glue (that has been dyed black) may be used to trace over the lead lines. The window should be cut out and hung where it will get plenty of sunlight.

Board: Use an overhead projector to enlarge the stained glass window. Cut a cross from each color paper listed and write the corresponding verse on it. Mount the crosses on the board so children will know what color to use when they have memorized a Bible verse.

B–Blue	Luke 23:43	b–Brown	Matthew 27:46
R–Red	John 19:28	G–Green	John 19:26-27
Y–Yellow	John 19:30	P–Purple	Luke 23:34

Color the outer rims of the cross and flowers white.   Luke 23:46

Activity: Visit churches to see stained glass windows. Discuss the symbols on them.

Book: *The New Testament in Stained Glass* (coloring book) by Pat Haeger, 1979, Scarlet Press

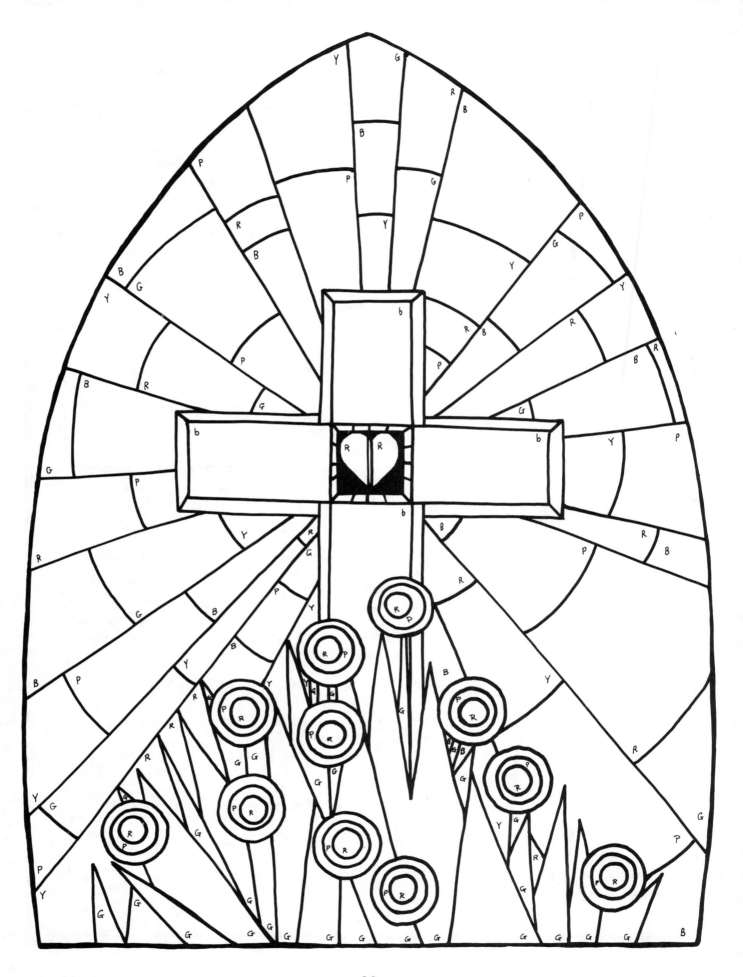

38

SS3810

APRIL FOOLS' DAY

A PROVERB A DAY
KEEPS FOOLISHNESS AWAY

APRIL

1	2	3	4	5	6	7
8	9	10	11	12	13	14
15	16	17	18	19	20	21
22	23	24	25	26	27	28
29	30					

Verse: "The lips of the wise spread knowledge; not so the hearts of fools."

Proverbs 15:7

Patterns: Copy page 40 for each child. Assign each a different proverb to write on the scroll. These proverbs pertain to fools: Proverbs 1:7; 1:22; 1:32; 3:35; 8:5; 10:1; 10:8; 10:21; 10:23; 11:29; 12:1; 12:16; 12:23; 13:19; 13:20; 14:3; 14:7; 14:8; 14:9; 14:16; 14:24; 15:2; 15:5; 15:7; 15:14; 16:22; 17:10; 17:16; 18:2; 19:1; 21:20; 23:9; 26:11; and 29:11.

Board: Use an overhead projector to enlarge the calendar on page 12. Write "April" on the calendar and fill in the dates. Each day ask a different child to add a scroll to the calendar. Have the child read the proverb on the scroll and tell what it means.

Activity: Have children imagine some pranks biblical characters might have played if April Fools' Day had been celebrated in biblical times. Discuss some tricks mentioned in the Bible, such as the serpent tricking Eve and Jacob getting Esau's blessing.

Reading: Proverbs 1:1-7

VERSE: _____

On the scroll, write the Bible verse listed above. Use fancy letters like the ones below. Cut out the scroll and then tell what the proverb means.

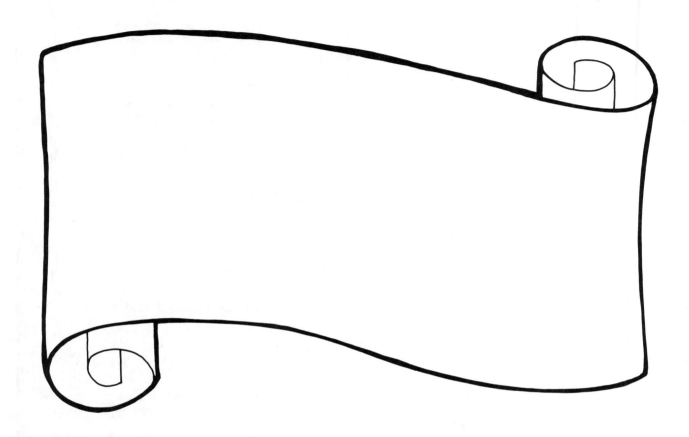

A B C D E F G H I J K L M N
O P Q R S T U V W X Y Z

a b c d e f g h i j k l m n
o p q r s t u v w x y z

SS3810

HELP SAVE THE EARTH

One person can make a difference.

Verse: "Two of every kind of bird, of every kind of animal and of every kind of creature that moves along the ground will come to you to be kept alive."
Genesis 6:20

Pattern: Copy the rainbow on page 42 for each child to color and cut out. Have each one write on the rainbow his promise to the earth. (Examples: I will pick up trash in my neighborhood once a week. I will recycle cans.)

Board: Use an overhead projector to enlarge the ark scene above, or display any pictures you may already have of Noah and the animals. Include a balloon blurb for Noah saying "One person can make a difference." Add the rainbow promises.

Activity: Help the class choose a project to do that will benefit the wonderful world God made, such as adopting a zoo animal that is on the endangered species list and helping to pay for its care with money earned from recycling or planting trees throughout the community.

Song: "Rise and Shine" with verses about Noah

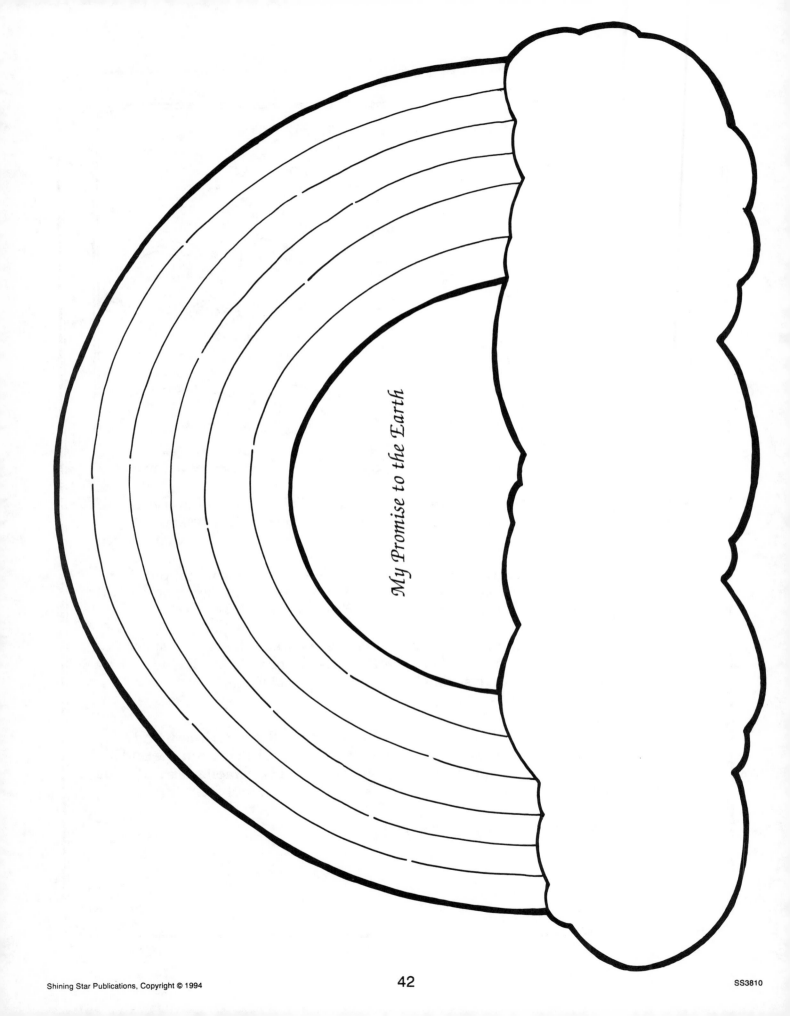

My Promise to the Earth

42

SS3810

EARTH DAY

RECYCLE YOUR PRAYERS FOR THE EARTH

Verse: "Come and see what God has done, how awesome his works in man's behalf!" Psalm 66:5

Pattern: Copy the pattern on page 44 for each child. Have him write on it a prayer thanking God for the many wonderful things on earth. Copy the scroll pattern on page 40 also. Have each child write on the scroll a prayer for the world. Encourage children to recycle (use) their prayers over and over again.

Board: Cut the letters for the board out of recycled paper. Alternate the children's scrolls and world patterns.

Activity: Let children form a circle symbolic of the earth. The first child says, "Thank You, God, for _____" (something that begins with "a"). The next child repeats the first child's prayer and adds something beginning with "b." The prayer is *recycled* over and over and continues building through the alphabet. If a child makes a memory mistake or is unable to think of a word to add to the list, the game continues with the next child.

Song: "He's Got the Whole World in His Hands"

SS3810

A WORLD OF THANKS TO GOD

SS3810

EARTH DAY

GOD BLESSED US WITH THE CARE OF ALL LIVING THINGS

Verse: "God blessed them and said to them, ' . . . Rule over the fish of the sea and the birds of the air and over every living creature that moves along the ground.'"
Genesis 1:28

Pattern: Help children research endangered species to fill in copies of the activity sheet on page 46.

Board: Use an overhead projector to enlarge the picture of Adam and Eve above for the center of the board. Add the children's completed activity pages to the bulletin board.

Activity: Watch a film about an endangered species or a threatened habitat. Pray that we may find ways to save it.

Songs: "Everything Is Beautiful"
"Handle with Care" (from the album *Sir Oliver's Song*)

· FRANCOLIN · GAUR · HARTEBEEST · IBEX · JAGUARUNDI · KAGU · LEMUR · MARGAY · NUMBAT · ORYX · PECCARY · PRONGHORN · QUOKKA · RHEA · SIKA · TAKIN · TAPIR · TUATARA · VIZCACHA · WALLABY · WATERBUCK · WOMBAT · YAK · ADDAX · ANOA · AYE-AYE · BANDICOOT · BELUGA · CAIMAN · CONDOR · DUIKER · ELAND

NAME ______________________________

There are many species of plants and animals in danger of becoming extinct. Draw an endangered plant or animal here.

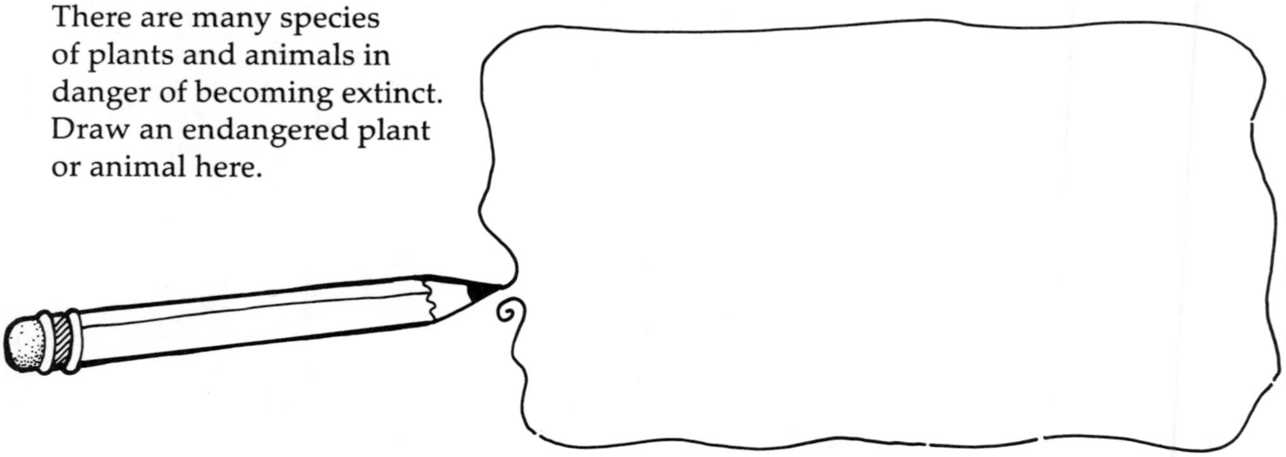

Describe the endangered species you have chosen and tell why it is endangered.

____

____

____

What can be done to help save this species?

____

____

____

Write a prayer for the endangered species you have chosen.

____

____

____

____

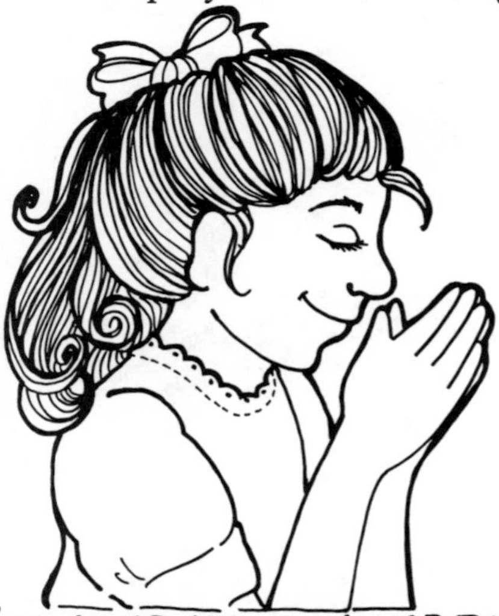

GOD SENDS THE SHOWERS THAT BRING MAY FLOWERS

Verse: "He has made everything beautiful in its time."   Ecclesiastes 3:11a

Patterns: Copy the flowers on page 48 for children to color and cut out. Have them punch small holes in each and string together to make leis.

Board: Cut letters from floral wallpaper or shelf liner. The children's leis may be pinned to the board in a pleasing arrangement. Add a few loose paper flowers.

Activity: Tell children that Lei Day is celebrated in Hawaii on the first day of May. Encourage them to find out about Hawaiian customs. Teach them a few Hawaiian words, such as *aloha*–hello, goodbye, love; *mahalo*–thanks; *aikane*–friend; *Pehea oe?*–How are you? Encourage children to memorize the Bible verses. At the end of the month, celebrate the children's efforts at memorization by having a classroom Lei Day. Take down the leis for all to wear and have a luau-type feast.

Song: "Love His Name" (This song contains Hawaiian words and is part of the album, *Sir Oliver's Song* by Sparrow Music.)

"All men are like grass and all their glory is like the flowers of the field."
Isaiah 40:6

"He has made everything beautiful in its time."
Ecclesiastes 3:11

"Many, O Lord my God, are the wonders you have done."
Psalm 40:5

"God saw all that he had made and it was very good."
Genesis 1:31

"The hills are clothed with gladness."
Psalm 65:12

"How many are your works, O Lord! In wisdom you made them all . . . ."
Psalm 104:24

"The grass withers and the flowers fall, but the word of our God stands forever."
Isaiah 40:8

"For by him all things were created."
Colossians 1:16

"Yet I tell you that not even Solomon in all his splendor was dressed like one of these."
Matthew 6:29

SS3810

MOTHER'S DAY MATCHUP

Verse: ". . . Parents are the pride of their children."   Proverbs 17:6

Patterns: Make a copy of page 50 for each child. Each one should color and cut out both frames. A picture of the child may be taped to one. A picture of her mother may be taped to the other.

Board: Display pictures of mothers and their children in mixed-up order. Let children try to guess which ones match. Change the pictures weekly during the month of May so everyone gets a turn.

Activity: Take a photo of each child to tape to one frame. On the other frame, have the child write a poem or letter to her mother. The frames may be given as Mother's Day gifts or used to make Mother's Day cards. The frame patterns may be used for other occasions; for example, a snapshot taken by you on a child's birthday can be sent home in the frame, or pictures of the children can be displayed with the caption "Welcome to Room ____."

Book: *Hooray for Mother's Day!* by Marjorie Sharmat, 1986, Holiday

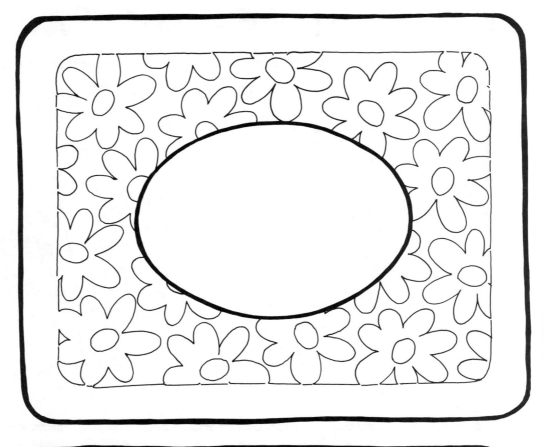

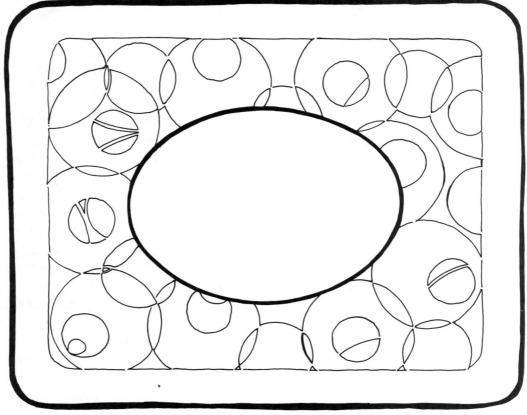

SS3810

WHAT MOMS ARE MADE OF

Verse: "She watches over the affairs of her household and does not eat the bread of idleness. Her children arise and call her blessed."

Proverbs 31:27-28a

Patterns: Copy page 52 for each child. Have the child color and cut out all the pieces, then write her name on the first blank line of the recipe card. Each child should list the recipe which makes her mom special, such as *Ingredients:* $1/4$ Tb patience, 1 cup of faith, 3 tsp sugary sweetness, 10 oz of energy for carpooling, $1/2$ cup creativity, 1 oz of compassion, a ton of love. *To make:* Mix well and add lots of hugs to get the best mom in the world. *Serves:* Our family night and day.

Board: Decorate the board with the children's recipe cards and baking tools. Real sugar boxes, spatulas, and measuring cups may be used as part of the display. If space permits, real recipe cards would make a nice border.

Activity: Children may use the patterns to make Mother's Day cards. Cookies could be made at school to give as a gift. The icing on the cookies could say "Mom" or "I Love You."

Prayer: Thank You, Lord, for the mother You made especially for me.

SS3810

RECIPE FROM: _____

INGREDIENTS: _____

_____

_____

_____

TO MAKE: _____

SERVES: _____

SPICE

SS3810

BOUQUETS FILLED WITH LOTS OF LOVE

FOR MOTHERS SENT FROM GOD ABOVE

Verse: "Dear children, let us not love with words or tongue but with actions and in truth." 1 John 3:18

Pattern: Copy the bouquet on page 54 for each child. On each flower of the bouquet, the child may write an action he will perform for his mother. (Examples: I will give you plenty of hugs and kisses. I will say a prayer for you. I will wash the dishes.) After filling out the gift tag, the child may color and cut out the bouquet.

Board: Mount the bouquets all over the board and add hearts and colorful letters that spell "MOM."

Activity: Teach children how to make tissue paper flowers with pipe cleaner stems. Let the children arrange the flowers in recycled containers they've decorated with material scraps, stickers, wallpaper samples, buttons, etc.

Prayer: Dear Lord, help me to appreciate all the things my mother does for me. Open my eyes to ways I can help her and show her how much I love her.

TO:

FROM:

54

SS3810

REMEMBERED

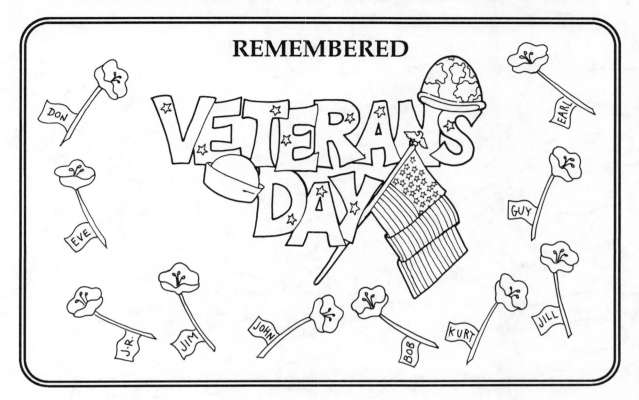

Verse: "The Lord gives strength to his people; the Lord blesses his people with peace." Psalm 29:11

Pattern: Make several copies of the poppy on page 56 for children to color and cut out. Children may write on the tags the names of people they wish to remember on this day. Allow them to use as many poppies as they need. Some children may want to leave their tags blank in memory of unknown soldiers.

Board: Use an overhead projector to enlarge the words "Memorial Day" or "Veterans Day" for the center of the board. Surround the name of the holiday with the children's poppies.

Activity: Pause for a moment of silence to pray for loved ones and for those who have died in the service of our country.

Reading: Psalm 23

56

SS3810

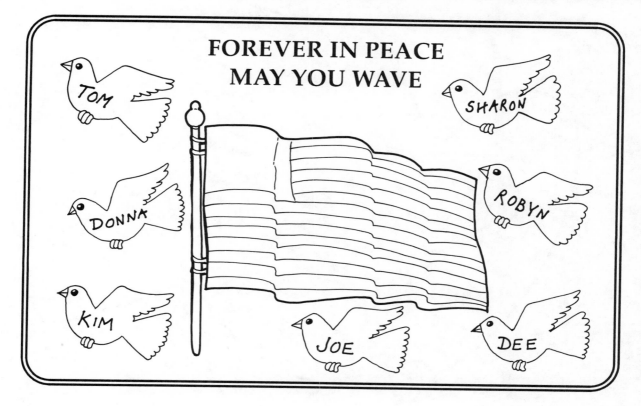

FOREVER IN PEACE MAY YOU WAVE

Verse: "... on earth peace to men ...."   Luke 2:14

Patterns: Copy the flag and dove on page 58 for children to color and cut out. Tape a straw to the flag to serve as a pole. Have children write their names on the doves.

Board: The letters for the caption should be colored with red, white, and blue stripes. Small toothpick flags, available from craft stores, may be used to form a border. Use an overhead projector to enlarge the flag for the center of the board. Add a narrow strip of paper to serve as the pole. After discussing ways the children can be messengers of peace, add their doves to the board. When the display is taken down, the children may pin the doves to their sleeves to remind them to be peacemakers.

Activity: Discuss our flag's history and symbolism and the proper way to display it. Have each child hold his flag while reciting the "Pledge of Allegiance" and singing "The Star-Spangled Banner." Each child may wave the flag proudly while singing "You're a Grand Old Flag."

Songs: "You're a Grand Old Flag"
"The Star-Spangled Banner"
"Let There Be Peace on Earth"

58

SS3810

DADS ARE SPECIAL

One of the best gifts
I've ever had,
Came from God.
I call him Dad.

Verse: "Honor your father and your mother."   Exodus 20:12a

Patterns: Copy page 60 for each child. Have the child decorate the word "DAD" with drawings and stickers that represent the interests of his father. These may include sports symbols, occupational symbols, pictures of hobbies, favorite foods, etc. Each child may write an appropriate award on the trophy: World's Greatest Hugger, Family's Greatest Chef, Best Dad. All the patterns should be colored and cut out.

Board: Use an overhead projector to enlarge the ribbon for the center of the board. Display the children's trophies and decorated words around it.

Activity: When taken down from the display, the words and trophies may be used to make Father's Day cards. The ribbons may be worn by the children on Father's Day. If possible, invite fathers to a ceremony in which they receive their cards and trophy awards.

Song: "For He's a Jolly Good Fellow"

One of the best gifts
I've ever had,
Came from God.
I call him Dad.

60

SS3810

FATHER'S DAY

YOU TAUGHT ME
THE WAY OF THE LORD

Verse: "Fathers, do not exasperate your children; instead, bring them up in the training and instruction of the Lord."
Ephesians 6:4

Patterns: Copy page 62 for the children. On the pattern of her choice, have each child list things her father has taught her, such as the importance of doing one's best, how to behave at church, or how to be kind to others. The patterns may also be used on other occasions to thank a teacher, secretary, computer aide, etc. When the patterns have been colored and cut out, they may be displayed or given to the appropriate people.

Board: The computers and chalkboards should be placed randomly on the board. Use the DAD pattern on page 60 and the male doll pattern on page 68 to make a border.

Activity: Help children make a banner that looks like a computerized printout that says "Happy Father's Day." Children may personalize the printout with their own artwork and signatures. Each child may write an unsigned Father's Day message on the board. Invite fathers to visit. Let each father guess which message was written by his child.

Prayer: Dear God, help me to see the wisdom of my father's words. Make me more willing to obey him as he tries to teach me what is right.

SS3810

SS3810

ONE NATION
UNDER
GOD,
INDIVISIBLE,

WITH LIBERTY
AND JUSTICE
FOR ALL

Verse: "Send forth your light and your truth, let them guide me."   Psalm 43:3a

Patterns: Copy page 64 for the children. On the torches, children may write Bible verses about light, liberty, truth, justice, etc. (Examples: Psalm 119:105; Matthew 5:16; John 8:12, 32; 14:6; Galatians 3:24.) Let children color and cut out both patterns.

Board: Make striped or solid letters of red, white, and blue for the caption. Use an overhead projector to enlarge the statue on page 64; then display the children's torches around it. Encourage them to memorize the verses on the torches.

Activity: Have children share a fact about the Statue of Liberty, such as it was given to the U.S. by the French to commemorate the 100th anniversary of American independence; it was dedicated on October 28, 1886. Have the children read the poem stanza on the statue together. Discuss how its message compares to Matthew 25:31-46. Encourage children to do what those verses say.

Reading: Matthew 25:31-46

Give me your tired, your poor,
Your huddled masses yearning
to breathe free,
The wretched refuse of your
teeming shore.
Send these, the homeless, tem-
pest-tost to me.
I lift my lamp beside the golden
door!

Emma Lazarus

64

GOD BLESS AMERICA,

LAND THAT I LOVE

Verse: "May the nations be glad and sing for joy, for you rule the people justly and guide the nations of the earth." Psalm 67:4

Patterns: Copy the patterns on page 66 for children to color, cut out, and glue to paper plates that have been colored with red, white, and blue designs. The star pattern may be traced over and over again to make stars for decorating the plates.

Board: Divide the board into two sections. Use an overhead projector to enlarge the bell, eagle, and star for the left half of the board. Invite children to bring postcards, calendar pictures, magazine photos, or drawings of U.S. scenery for the right half of the board. Make striped or solid red, white, and blue letters. Use the children's patriotic paper plates to form a border, or display them near the board.

Activity: Show slides of national parks and other scenic places in America as the patriotic music listed below is played. After the presentation, thank God for the scenic wonders He created and ask Him to bless America.

Songs: "God Bless America"
"America, the Beautiful"
"This Land Is Your Land"

"But those who hope in the Lord
will renew their strength.
They will soar on wings like eagles."

Isaiah 40:31a

". . . proclaim liberty throughout
the land to all its inhabitants."
Leviticus 25:10a

66

HOLD ONTO FRIENDSHIP

Verse: "A friend loves at all times." Proverbs 17:17a

Patterns: Copy page 68 for each child. Reproduce the patterns on paper of many different colors, or have the children cut them out and trace them on colored paper. Have the children add silver glitter to some of the paper dolls and gold glitter to others.

Board: Cut out large letters to spell FRIENDS. Leave the letters plain or cover them with magazine pictures of people of all sizes, ages, and nationalities. Display the paper dolls and hearts around the word FRIENDS. The dolls may also be used as a border.

Activity: Form a circle and hold hands while you sing the following Girl Scout song in unison or as a round. (If you aren't familiar with the tune, ask a Brownie or Girl Scout.)
"Make new friends but keep the old.
One is silver and the other's gold."

Songs: "Make New Friends"
"Let's Be Friends with One Another"

68

LABOR DAY

LABOR DAY . . . WHAT MIGHT THEY PRAY?

Lord, Give me food for my soul, that I might feed others.

Lord, guide my steps in the way of grace.

God, thank You for a colorful world.

Lord, Make my classroom a place where learning comes to life. ABC

Lord, Give me courage and strength.

Dear God, Give me a heart of compassion and hands of skill to treat my patients.

Dear Lord, Give me the input to output more.

Lord, Help me to be like the wise builder.

Verse: "There are different kinds of working, but the same God works all of them in all men." 1 Corinthians 12:6

Patterns: Enlarge each occupational symbol on page 70 to be the size of the patterns on page 62. Make a few copies of each symbol, including the computer and chalkboard from page 62. (If you are unable to enlarge the patterns, glue each small pattern to the corner of a large note card.) Have each child choose a symbol and write on it a prayer that might be said by someone in the occupation symbolized.

Board: Display the symbols on which the children have written. You may want to decorate the board with real objects that relate to the occupations portrayed, such as Band-aids™, paintbrush, nails, chalk, cookie cutter, police badge, or floppy disk.

Activity: Invite parents and other members of the community to talk to the children about their work. Pray for the guests and send them thank-you notes for the services they perform.

Reading: 1 Corinthians 12

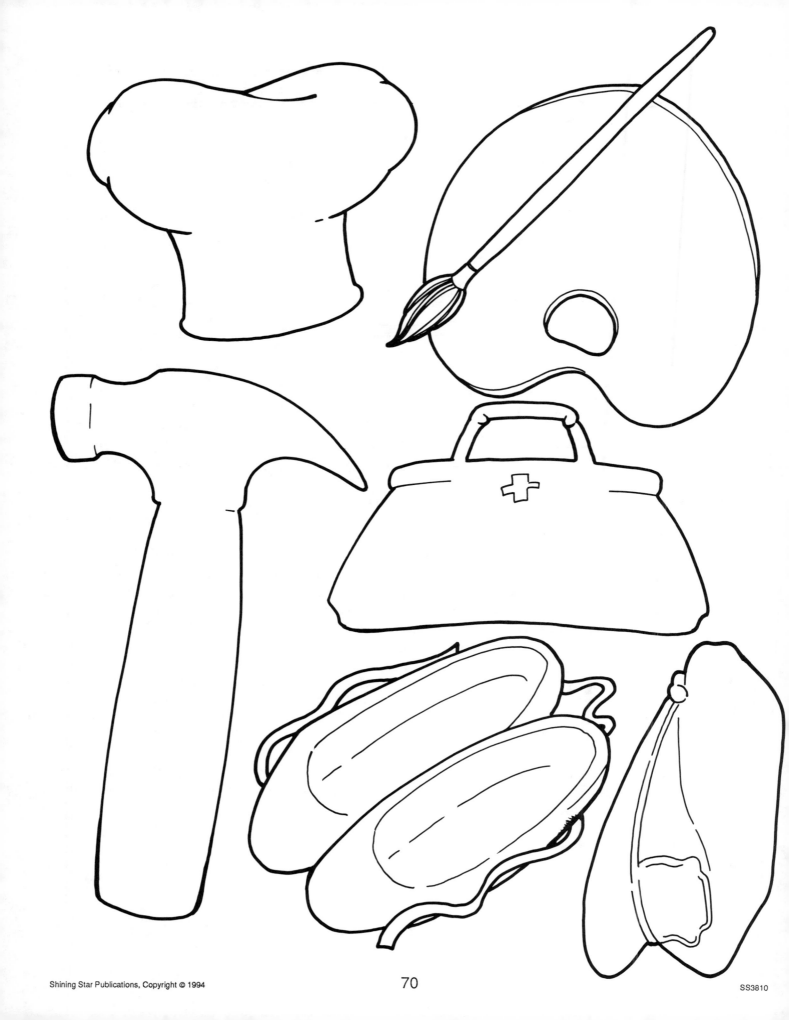

SS3810

I CAN USE MY GIFTS
TO SERVE THE LORD

Verse: "Always give yourselves fully to the work of the Lord, because you know that your labor in the Lord is not in vain."   1 Corinthians 15:58b

Patterns: Copy page 72 for each child. Have the child write his name after "To." On each crayon in the box, the child may write a God-given gift. In the crayon frame, have the child draw or list a way to use each gift to be of service. (Example: I can use my artistic talent to make a card for someone who is lonely.) Have children color and cut out the patterns.

Board: Use an overhead projector to enlarge the box of crayons. Display the children's crayon boxes and frames around it. Cut the letters out of several basic colors. Use the single crayon pattern to reproduce crayons of basic colors for the border, or tape real crayons to any border you choose.

Activity: Wrap a box of crayons and ask a child to open the gift. Explain that each crayon is different, but each is important in the making of a picture. In the same way, each child has different talents. Each child is important and can serve the Lord in his or her own way. As a new school year begins, it is important to accept differences among classmates and to find ways to use individual gifts for the good of all.

Reading: 1 Corinthians 12

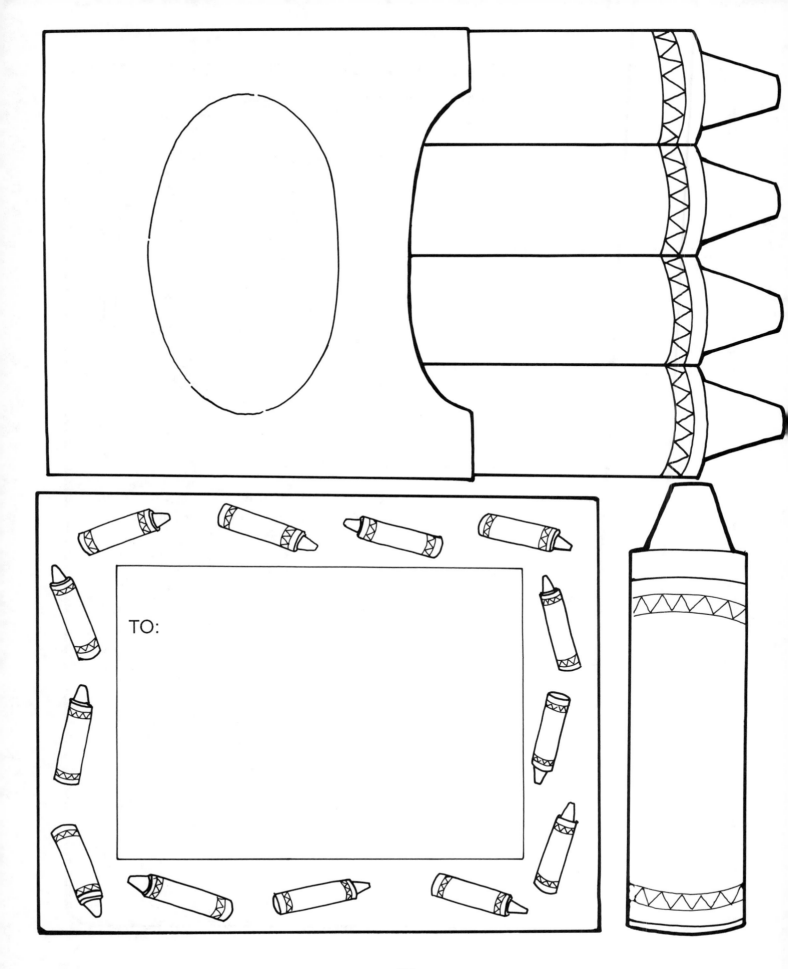

TO:

SS3810

GRANDPARENTS ARE
A GIFT FROM GOD

Verse: "Children's children are a crown to the aged."   Proverbs 17:6a

Pattern: Have each child interview a grandparent to ask about memorable child-hood moments, favorite things to do with grandchildren, and special moments in his or her life. Copy page 74 for each child to use, writing a newspaper article for each heading and drawing a picture to go with it.

Board: Display the children's news sheets with any pictures they have of the grandparents they interviewed. Cut the letters for the caption out of black and white newsprint or colored comics. Outline the letters with a black marker.

Activity: Have the children make posters or cards for their grandparents that say the following:
"God wanted to give children a very special gift,
So He gave them grandparents!"

Prayer: Encourage each child to complete this prayer aloud:
"My grand ____ is special because ____. Thank You, Lord, for making him (her) special."

THE GRAND TIMES

"...Future generations will be told about the Lord." Psalm 22:30

GRAND MEMORIES OF CHILDHOOD

_____
_____
_____
_____
_____

GRAND TIMES WITH GRANDCHILDREN

_____
_____
_____
_____
_____

GRAND MOMENTS IN LIFE

_____
_____
_____
_____
_____

SS3810

U.N. DAY/CHILDREN'S DAY

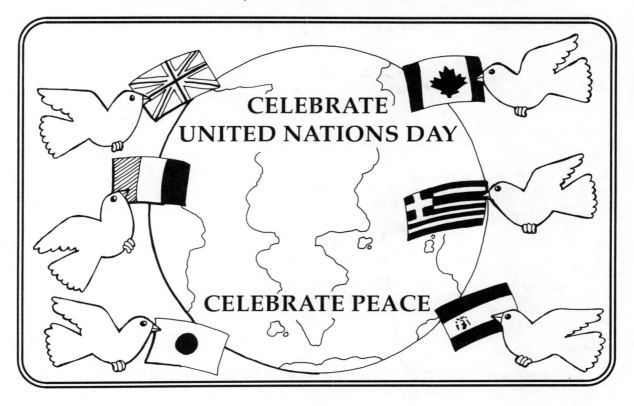

CELEBRATE
UNITED NATIONS DAY

CELEBRATE PEACE

Verse: "Let the peace of Christ rule in your hearts, since as members of one body you were called to peace." Colossians 3:15

Patterns: Make copies of page 76 for all the children. Help them research the colors of these flags, color and cut out. In addition, flags of other United Nations countries may be drawn and used. Each child will also need to cut out a dove made from the pattern on page 58.

Board: Use an overhead projector to enlarge the earth pattern on page 44. Around the earth, display each child's dove carrying a flag. The remaining flags may be used to form a border.

Activity: Teach the children about the history and purpose of the United Nations. Have a flag parade, letting each child carry one of his flags attached to a straw while singing songs about peace and brotherhood.

Songs: "Let There Be Peace on Earth"
"May the Peace of the Lord Be with You"

SS3810

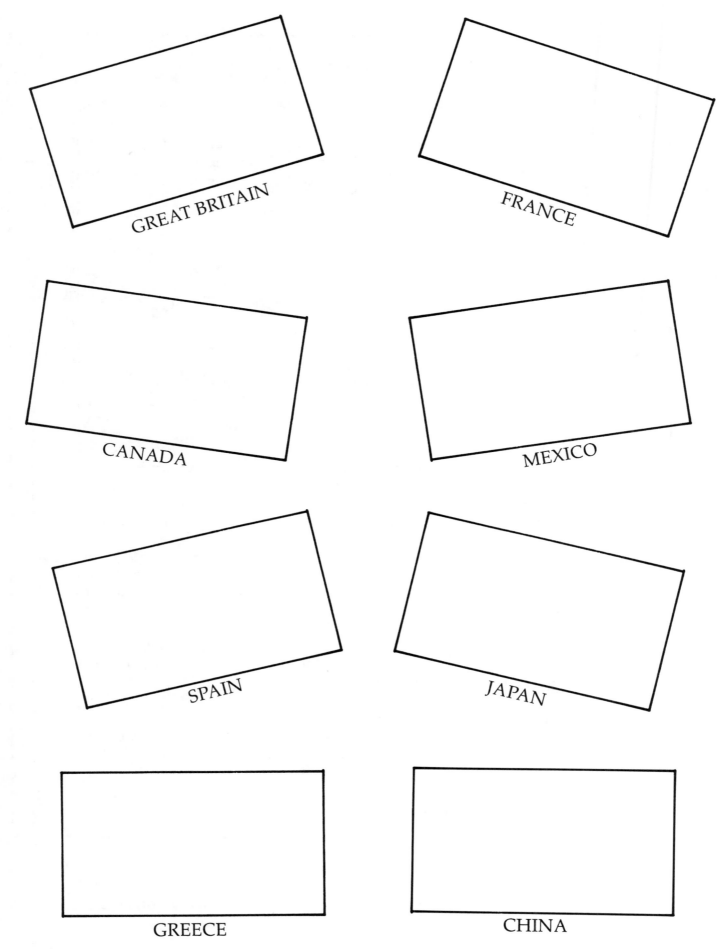

GREAT BRITAIN

FRANCE

CANADA

MEXICO

SPAIN

JAPAN

GREECE

CHINA

76

SS3810

CHILDREN EVERYWHERE
HONOR HIS NAME

YAHOVA

DIOS

BOŽE

GOD

神

ALLAH

Verse: "We are God's children."   Romans 8:16b

Patterns: Copy page 78 for each child. After talking about each of the countries portrayed by the paper dolls, have children color and cut out the figures.

Board: Use an overhead projector to enlarge the earth pattern on page 44. Display the paper dolls around the world and elsewhere on the board. Add the name for God in several languages. If desired, use the flags from page 76 as a border.

Activity: Allow children to dress in international costumes. Teach them to say a few words in other languages, and discuss the customs and traditions of various countries. Let them sing along to the music of *Sir Oliver's Song,* a collection of songs about the Ten Commandments, published by Sparrow Music. The musical includes words from several different languages.

Songs: "Up, Up with People"
"Let There Be Peace on Earth"
"What Color Is God's Skin?"
"Everybody Needs Jesus"

MEXICO

SCOTLAND

NETHERLANDS

JAPAN

NIGERIA

CHINA

SS3810

Whooo knows some words to the wise?

PUMPKIN PATCH OF PROVERBS

PROVERBS 11:24
PROVERBS 27:2
PROVERBS 17:22
PROV...
PROVERBS 18:5
PROVERBS 22:1

Verse: "Pay attention and listen to the sayings of the wise; apply your heart to what I teach."
Proverbs 22:17

Pattern: Copy the pumpkin on page 80 on orange paper for each child, or have children color the pumpkins orange and cut them out. Have each child write a favorite Bible verse from Proverbs on the pumpkin. Appropriate verses include: Proverbs 3:5; 11:24; 12:16; 13:20; 14:21; 15:1; 16:3; 16:8; 17:22; 18:5; 19:17; 19:20; 21:13; 22:1; 27:1; and 27:2.

Board: Use an overhead projector to enlarge the owl shown above. Display the owl in a corner of the board. Use the children's pumpkins to create a pumpkin patch at the bottom of the board.

Activity: Each child may "pick" a pumpkin verse to memorize each day or week. Encourage all the children to learn as many verses as possible for a bountiful harvest.

Prayer: Dear God, give me the wisdom to understand Your teachings.

SS3810

80

SS3810

ELECT TO BE A MEMBER
OF GOD'S PARTY

CHOOSE GOD!

GOD PROMISES YOU
THE KINGDOM

HIS WAY IS...
THE RIGHT WAY!

Verse: "Therefore, my brothers, be all the more eager to make your calling and election sure." 2 Peter 1:10a

Patterns: Copy page 82 for all the children. After telling them that the donkey and elephant are symbols of major political parties, have the children draw symbols on the buttons to represent God's "party." (Examples: angel, dove, lamb, etc.) On the bumper sticker, each child may write a slogan or verse to help persuade someone to become a member of God's "party." The child may write on the ribbon a "campaign promise" or Bible verse telling of God's promises to those who follow His ways.

Board: Twist red, white, and blue streamers for a border. Cut the letters from red, white, and blue paper and display the bumper stickers, buttons, and ribbons.

Activity: Have children think of a theme song for God's "party."

Prayer: Dear God, help me to always elect or choose Your way. Grant me the courage to do what's right, especially when many around me choose a different path.

BUMPER STICKER

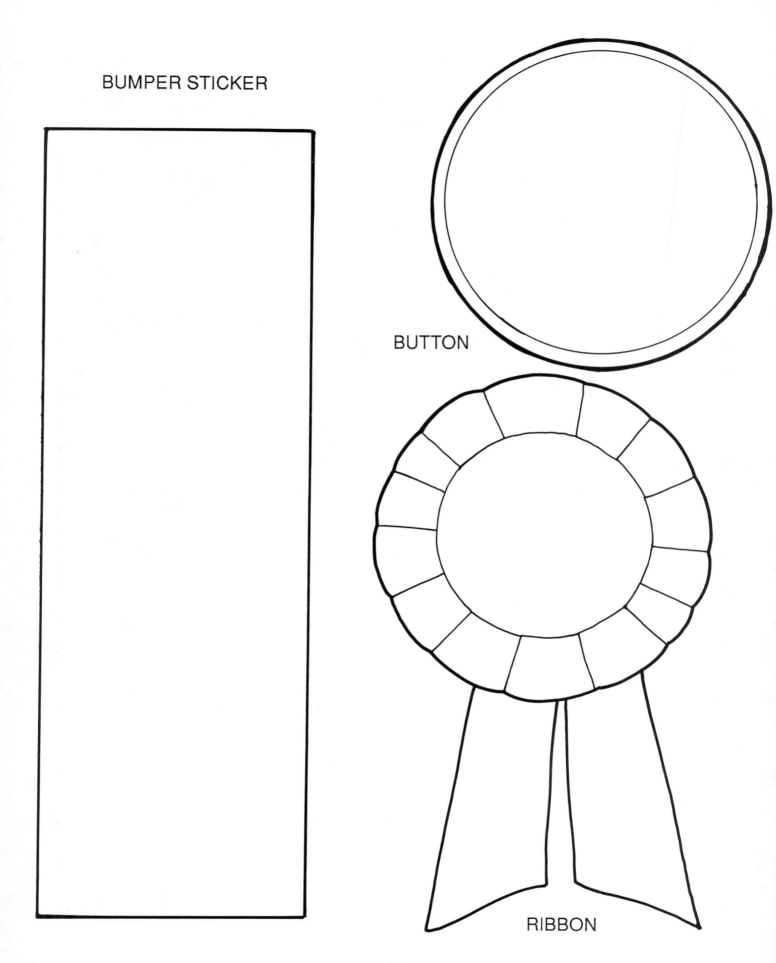

BUTTON

RIBBON

SS3810

THANKSGIVING

BLESS US, O LORD, AND THESE THY GIFTS

Verse: "When you have eaten and are satisfied, praise the Lord your God for the good land he has given you." Deuteronomy 8:10

Patterns: Copy page 84 for each child. Have the child write on the food things for which he is thankful; then color and cut them out. You may prefer to have each one write a Thanksgiving prayer or verse, such as Psalm 68:10 or Deuteronomy 8:10 on each pattern.

Board: Use an overhead projector to enlarge the picture of the feast shown above. Alternate the turkey and corn patterns to form a border. For the caption, cut letters from fall colors.

Activity: Serve a feast of corn bread, berries, and other foods the Pilgrims and Indians might have eaten. Teach children to say several different prayers for grace; then invite them to offer spontaneous prayers of thanksgiving.

Songs: "Now Thank We All Our God"
"Thank You, Lord"
"If I Were a Butterfly"

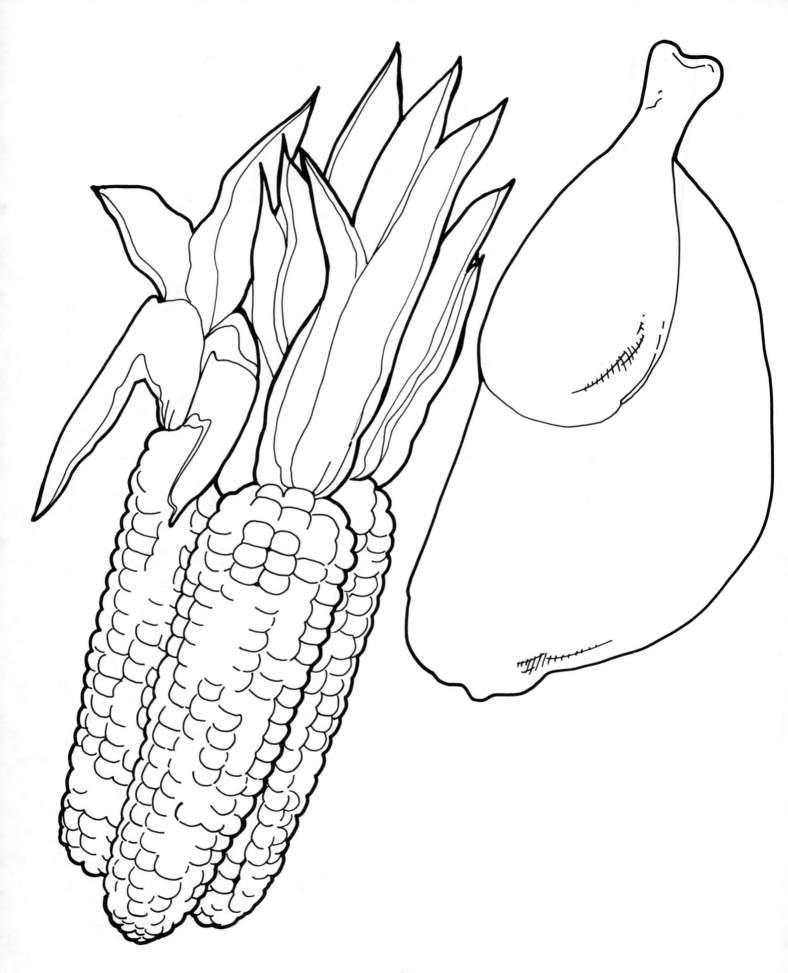

84

SS3810

Verse: "Give thanks to the Lord, for he is good; his love endures forever."
Psalm 107:1

Patterns: Reproduce page 86 on brown, yellow, red, and orange paper for children to cut out, or let them color the leaves with crayons. Have each child write something on each leaf for which she is thankful.

Board: Use the leaves to form a border. Cut the letters from fall colors. Use an overhead projector to enlarge the pilgrims shown above. Make several orange copies of the pumpkin on page 80. Write on each one a verse of thanksgiving, such as 1 Corinthians 15:57; Isaiah 12:4; or 1 Chronicles 16:8. You may prefer to use an expression of thanks to God in another language: for example, *Gracias a Dios, Grazie a Dio, and Hodo Li Yahova.* Change pumpkins after everyone has memorized what is on the one displayed.

Activity: Have children cover thin, white paper with splotches of red, orange, yellow, and green watercolors. Let them trace the leaf patterns on black paper, and cut them out. The remaining black paper may be glued on top of the painted one and placed in a window in the sunlight.

Song: "Now Thank We All Our God"

SS3810

FROM THY BOUNTY

Verse: "Your generosity will result in thanksgiving to God. This service that you perform is not only supplying the needs of God's people but is also over-flowing in many expressions of thanks to God."

2 Corinthians 9:11b-12

Patterns: Make copies of the food on page 88 for children to color and cut out.

Board: Use an overhead projector to enlarge the cornucopia shown above. Store the children's food patterns in a large envelope tacked to the board. Place a large, sturdy box decorated with a few of the children's food shapes on the floor.

Activity: Ask the children to collect canned goods or to buy food for the hungry with money they've earned themselves. Each time a child brings in a nonperishable food item and puts it into the box, he may select a paper food from the envelope to staple or pin to the board. Soon the board and the box will be overflowing with food. Donate the box of food to a local charity that helps to feed the hungry.

Reading: 2 Corinthians 9:6-15

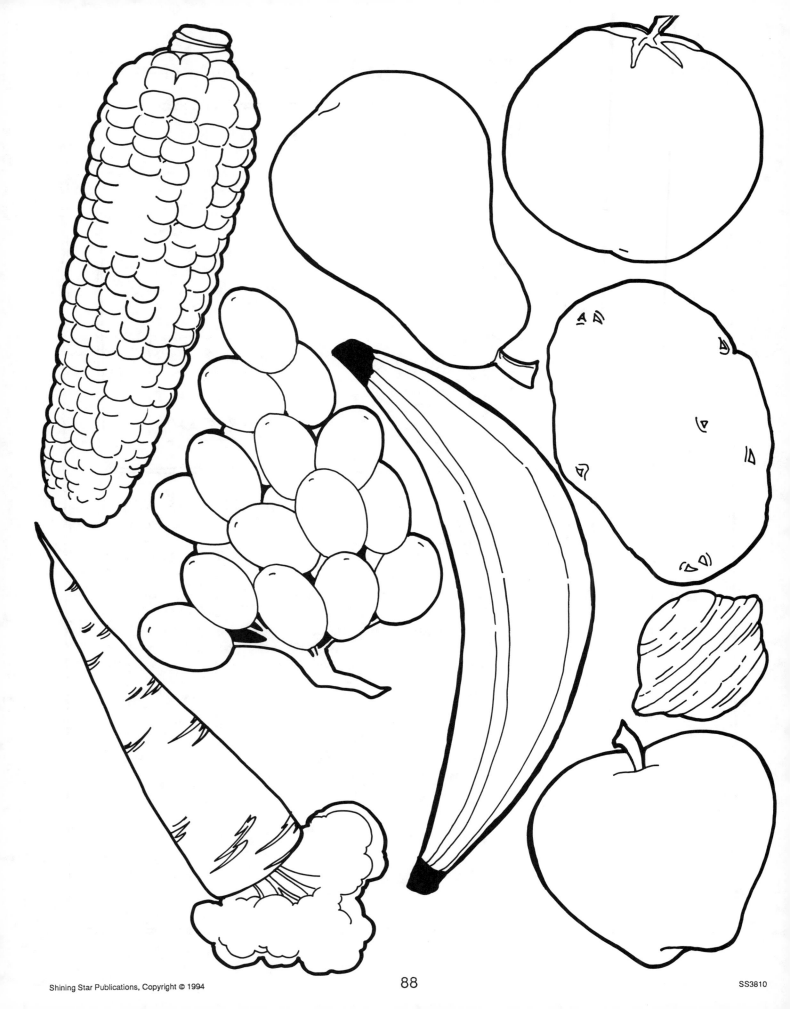

SS3810

ALL THE WORLD AWAITS HIS LIGHT

Verse: "The people walking in darkness have seen a great light."   Isaiah 9:2a

Patterns: Copy the candles on page 90 for children to color, cut out, and decorate with glitter, tissue paper balls, bric-a-brac, sequins, doily pieces, and other scraps. Children may wish to write Bible verses, such as John 8:12; Isaiah 2:5; 9:2; or 60:1 on their candles. If space permits, the paper dolls on page 78 may also be colored and cut out for use on this Advent board.

Board: Use an overhead projector to enlarge the world pattern on page 44. Display the children's candles around it. Add paper dolls, if desired. Optional captions include "May the Peace of Christ's Coming Warm Our Hearts" or "Come, Lord Jesus. Come and Be Born in Our Hearts." Hearts may replace the world at the center of the board.

Activity: Place an Advent wreath near the board. Gather children around it for Advent readings (such as Isaiah 9:1-7), celebrations, and songs. Encourage children to carry the warmth of Christ's light in their hearts for all the world to see. Discuss some *shining* deeds they can do this Christmas.

Songs: "O Come, O Come, Emmanuel"
"The Light of Christ"
"This Little Light of Mine"

SS3810

A CHRISTMAS PLEDGE

When visions of sugarplums dance in my head, I'll remember sweet Jesus on His manger bed.

Verse: "Taste and see that the Lord is good."   Psalm 34:8a

Patterns: Copy page 92 for children to color and cut out. Have them cut off two corners of yellow, orange, red, or light green construction paper, as shown, to make house shapes. They may use the sweets to decorate their houses and add cotton for snow.

Board: Use an overhead projector to enlarge the scroll on page 40. Decorate it with sweets and write the Christmas pledge on it. Display the children's houses around the pledge. A border of gingerbread people cut from brown paper may be added. Add a few drops of red or green food coloring to some bottles of glue, stir well, and let children enjoy icing the gingerbread people with the glue.

Activity: Remind the children to look past the decorations, toys, and treats to the real reason for this season. Have a birthday party for Jesus. After singing "Happy Birthday," have children recite the Christmas pledge together. Then serve birthday treats.

Songs: "Happy Birthday to You"
"Away in a Manger"
"Christmas Lullaby"

When visions of
sugarplums
dance in
my head,
I'll remember
sweet Jesus
on His
manger bed.

REPEAT THE SOUNDING JOY

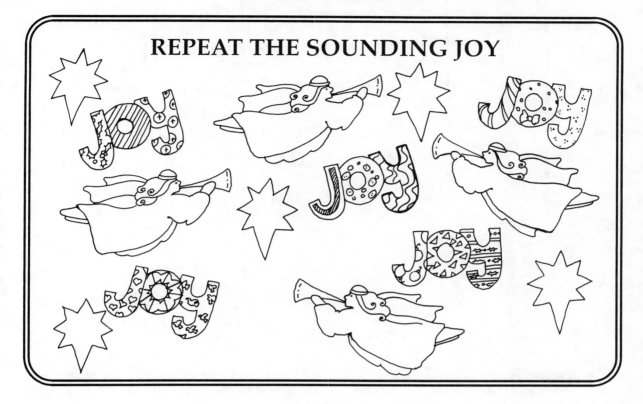

Verse: "But the angel said to them, 'Do not be afraid. I bring you good news of great joy that will be for all people. Today in the town of David, a Savior has been born to you; he is Christ the Lord.'" Luke 2:10-11

Patterns: Copy page 94 and the star on page 96 for children to cut out. The word JOY may be covered with wrapping paper or decorated with Christmas symbols, stickers, glitter, sequins, etc. Angels and stars may be covered with foil or decorated with glitter.

Board: Arrange the angels, words, and stars below the caption.

Activity: Children may use the patterns to make Christmas cards. Let this be one of the many ways you encourage them to spread the joy of Christ's birth.

Songs: "Joy to the World"
"Children, Run Joyfully"
"Go Tell It on the Mountain"

93

SS3810

SS3810

WHAT GIFT CAN I GIVE?

Verse: "Every good and perfect gift is from above, coming down from the Father of the heavenly lights."
James 1:17a

Patterns: Copy page 96 for children to color and cut out. Have each write on the star a gift to give from the heart. Use a cotton ball to spread cooking or mineral oil over the stained glass window to make it more translucent. When dry, it may be colored with crayons and hung in a window.

Board: Use an overhead projector to enlarge the stained glass window. Surround it with the children's stars. Have the children face the board as they pray, "Dear God, help us to be shining stars for You and to give of ourselves."

Activity: Read Matthew 2:1-12 and discuss the gifts brought by the wise men. Read legends of gifts to Baby Jesus, such as the Drummer Boy's gift of music, the Mexican child's poinsettia, and the Littlest Angel's box of earthly treasures. Explain that the best gifts are those from the heart. Have children make greeting cards, using their stained glass windows. The star may be glued inside each card and the child may write on it a gift from the heart that she will give to the recipient of the card.

Songs: "The Little Drummer Boy"   "What Can I Give Him?"
"This Little Light of Mine"   "We Three Kings"

SS3810

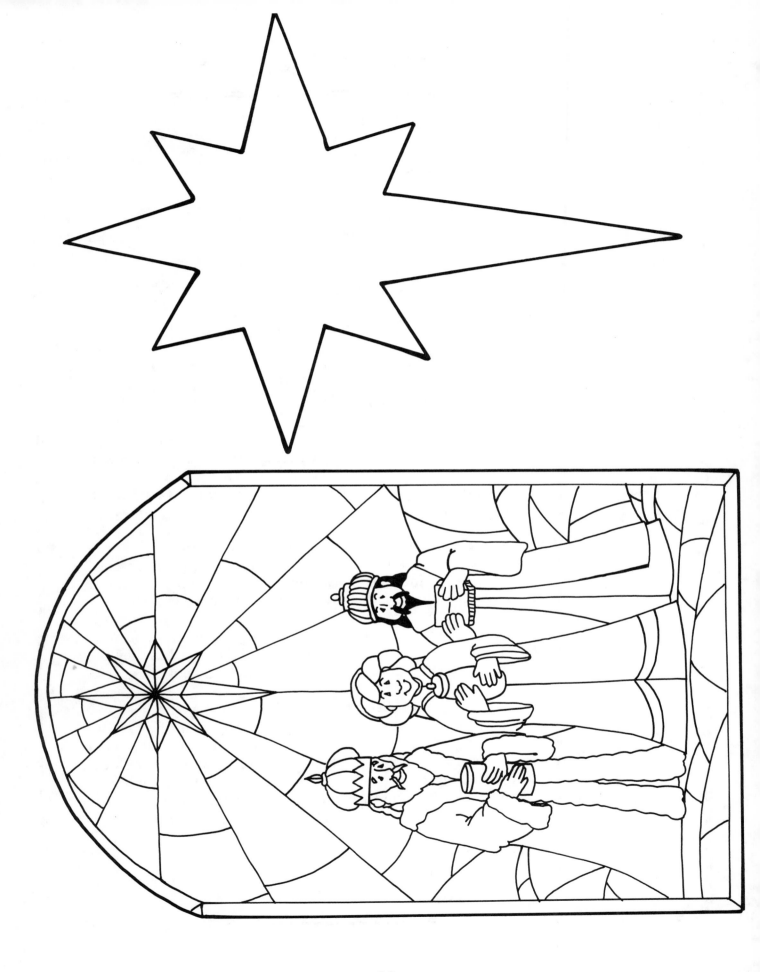

96

SS3810